# RETIRE EARLY

# WITH

# REAL ESTATE

## A Comprehensive Guide to Profitable Property Investments, Financial Independence, Wealth Building, Passive Income Strategies.

# J. B. BLACKWOOD

# TABLE OF CONTENT

Introduction ............................................................................ 5

Chapter 1: The Benefits of Real Estate Investing ........................ 7

Chapter 2: How to Get Started with Real Estate Investing ............ 9

Chapter 3: Financing Your Real Estate Investments .................... 18

Chapter 4: Building Your Real Estate Portfolio .......................... 22

Chapter 5: Managing Your Real Estate Investments .................... 24

Chapter 6: Maximizing Your Real Estate Returns ....................... 28

Chapter 7: Retiring Early with Real Estate ................................ 30

Conclusion ............................................................................. 33

Gratitude & Acknowledgment: ................................................. 35

# Introduction

John and Jane were a young couple who were tired of their 9-5 jobs and wanted to retire early. They had heard about real estate investing and decided to give it a try.

They started small by investing in a single rental property. They quickly realized that real estate investing was not as easy as it seemed. They had to deal with tenants, repairs, and maintenance. However, they persisted and gained knowledge from their errors.

Over time, John and Jane built a portfolio of rental properties. They were able to generate enough passive income to retire early and live the life they had always dreamed of. They traveled the world, spent time with family and friends, and pursued their passions.

John and Jane's success story is a testament to the power of real estate investing. With hard work, dedication, and a little bit of luck, anyone can retire early with real estate.

Are you tired of the daily grind and looking for a way to retire early? Do you want to be financially independent and lead a life that suits you? If so, you should read this book!

Retire Early with Real Estate is a comprehensive guide to help you achieve financial independence using real estate investments. In this book, you'll learn how to get started with real estate investing, finance your investments, build your portfolio, manage your investments, and maximize your returns. You'll also discover how to retire early with real estate and live the life you've always dreamed of.

The book is divided into nine chapters. In the first chapter, we'll introduce you to the concept of retiring early with real estate and explain why it's a smart investment strategy. In the second chapter, we'll explore the benefits of real estate investing and how it can help you achieve financial freedom. In the third chapter, we'll show you how to get started with real estate investing and provide tips for finding the right properties. In the fourth chapter, we'll discuss financing your real estate investments and provide guidance on how to secure funding. In the fifth chapter, we'll explain how to build your real estate portfolio and provide strategies for diversifying your investments. In the sixth chapter, we'll discuss managing your real estate investments and provide tips for maximizing your returns. In the seventh chapter, we'll show you how to maximize your real estate returns and provide guidance on how to sell your properties. In the eighth chapter, we'll explore how to retire early with real estate and provide strategies for achieving financial independence. Finally, in the ninth chapter, we'll conclude the book and provide some final thoughts on retiring early with real estate.

# Chapter 1: The Benefits of Real Estate Investing

Real estate investing has numerous benefits that make it an attractive investment option. Here are some of the key benefits of real estate investing:

1. Cash flow: Real estate investments can generate a steady stream of passive income through rental income. This income can be used to pay down your mortgage and build equity over time.

2. Tax advantages: Real estate investors can take advantage of numerous tax breaks and deductions that can save money at tax time. For example, you can deduct the reasonable costs of owning, operating, and managing a property. You can also depreciate the cost of buildings over their useful life, which can help lower your taxed income.

3. Appreciation: Real estate values tend to increase over time, and with a good investment, you can turn a profit when it's time to sell. Additionally, rents often increase over time, which may result in increased income flow.

4. Build equity and wealth: As you pay down a property mortgage, you build equity—an asset that's part of your net worth. Plus, when

you accumulate equity, you'll have the money to acquire more properties, which will boost your wealth and cash flow even further.

5. Portfolio diversification: Real estate has a low correlation with other major asset classes, which means the addition of real estate to a portfolio of diversified assets can lower portfolio increase in return for each unit of risk and volatility.

6. Inflation hedge: Real estate investments can act as a hedge against inflation. As inflation rises, so do rents and property values, which can help protect your investment returns.

7. Control: Real estate investments give you more control over your investment than other asset classes. You can choose the property, the location, the tenants, and the management of the property.

8. Leverage: Real estate investments can be leveraged, which means you can use other people's money to finance your investment. By doing this, you may be able to buy more houses and make more money.

9. Stable cash flow: Real estate investments can provide a stable source of cash flow, which can help you achieve financial independence and retire early.

10. Social benefits: Real estate investments can have social benefits such as providing affordable housing, creating jobs, and revitalizing neighborhoods.

# Chapter 2: How to Get Started with Real Estate Investing

Real estate investing is a popular and potentially profitable way to diversify your portfolio and generate income. However, getting started with real estate investing can be challenging, especially for beginners. The following stages will assist you in beginning your real estate investing career:

1. Identify your financial stage and goals. Before you invest in real estate, you need to have a clear idea of your current financial situation and your long-term objectives. How much money do you have to invest? How much risk can you tolerate? What sort of results are you seeking? What is the extent of your willingness to put in time and effort into your investments? These questions will help you narrow down your options and choose a strategy that suits your needs and preferences.

2. Choose a specific real estate investing strategy. There are many ways to invest in real estate, each with its own advantages and disadvantages. Some of the most common strategies are:

Rental properties: This involves buying and owning physical properties and renting them out to tenants.

You can earn income from rent and appreciation, but you also have to deal with maintenance, vacancies, and tenant issues. Rental properties require a lot of capital, time, and management skills.

Flipping: This involves buying undervalued or distressed properties, fixing them up, and selling them for a profit. You can make money quickly, but you also have to deal with renovation costs, market risks, and taxes. Flipping requires a lot of research, expertise, and cash flow.

Real estate investment trusts (REITs): These enterprises are those that own and manage properties that generate revenue, like hotels, malls, offices, and flats. You can buy shares of REITs through a brokerage account, similar to investing in stocks. You can earn dividends and capital gains, but you also have to pay fees and taxes. REITs offer liquidity, diversification, and passive income, but they also have lower control and potential conflicts of interest.

Online real estate platforms: These are websites that connect investors to real estate projects, such as crowdfunding, peer-to-peer lending, or syndication. You can invest in various types of properties and deals, often with lower minimums and fees than traditional methods. You can access more opportunities and information, but you also have to deal with platform risks, regulations, and due diligence.

3. Pick a target market and niche. Once you have a strategy, you need to decide where and what to invest in. You should research and analyze different markets and niches, such as location, property type, price range, demand, supply, competition, etc. You should look for markets and niches that have strong fundamentals, growth potential, and competitive advantages. You should also consider your personal preferences, experience, and network.

4. Decide your investment property criteria and budget. After you have a market and niche, you need to define your investment property criteria and budget. You should have a clear idea of what kind of properties you are looking for, such as size, condition, features, amenities, etc. You should also have a realistic estimate of how much money you can afford to spend, including purchase price, closing costs, repairs, holding costs, etc. You should use tools such as calculators, spreadsheets, and apps to help you crunch the numbers and evaluate the profitability of potential deals.

5. Build your team and network. Investing in real estate requires teamwork. You need to have a team and network of professionals and experts who can help you with various aspects of your investments, such as finding, financing, closing, managing, and selling properties. Some of the key people you may need are:

Real estate agent: A licensed professional who can help you find, negotiate, and buy properties. They can also provide you with market data, comps, and referrals.

Lender: A financial institution or individual who can provide you with loans or mortgages to finance your properties. They can also offer you different types of financing options, such as conventional, hard money, private money, etc.

Contractor: A skilled worker or company who can perform repairs, renovations, or improvements on your properties. They can also give you estimates, bids, and timelines for your projects.

Property manager: A person or company who can handle the day-to-day operations of your rental properties, such as finding and screening tenants, collecting rent, handling maintenance, resolving issues, etc. They can also save you time, hassle, and money in the long run.

Accountant: A certified professional who can help you with the tax and accounting aspects of your real estate investments, such as preparing and filing tax returns, maximizing deductions, minimizing liabilities, etc. They can also advise you on the best legal and financial structures for your business.

Attorney: A licensed professional who can help you with the legal aspects of your real estate investments, such as drafting and reviewing contracts, deeds, leases, etc. They can also protect you from lawsuits, disputes, and liabilities.

Mentor: An experienced and successful real estate investor who can guide you, teach you, and support you in your journey. They can also provide you with valuable insights, tips, and feedback.

Partner: A person or entity who can join you in your real estate investments, either as a co-owner, lender, borrower, or service provider. They can also provide you with additional capital, skills, resources, or connections.

6. Line up financing and raise cash. Before you start looking for properties, you need to have your financing and cash ready. You should have a pre-approval letter from your lender, which shows how much money you can borrow and at what terms. You should also have enough cash for your down payment, closing costs, and reserves. You can raise cash by saving, selling, borrowing, or partnering with others. You should also have multiple financing sources and backup plans in case your primary source falls through.

7. Create a plan to find deals. Finding good deals is one of the most important and challenging aspects of real estate investing. You need to have a plan to find deals that meet your criteria and budget, and

that offer you a good return on your investment. You can find deals by using various methods, such as:

Online sources: You can use websites, apps, and platforms that list properties for sale, such as MLS, Zillow, Trulia, Realtor.com, etc. You can also use online real estate platforms that offer exclusive or off-market deals, such as Fundrise, Roofstock, CrowdStreet, etc.

Offline sources: You can use traditional methods, such as newspapers, magazines, flyers, signs, etc., that advertise properties for sale. You can also use direct mail, cold calling, or door knocking to contact potential sellers directly.

Networking: You can use your team and network to help you find deals, such as asking for referrals, recommendations, or leads from your real estate agent, lender, contractor, property manager, accountant, attorney, mentor, partner, etc. You can also join and attend local or online real estate groups, clubs, associations, events, etc., where you can meet and connect with other investors, sellers, or professionals.

Marketing: You can use various strategies, such as branding, advertising, social media, etc., to promote yourself and your business, and to attract and generate leads from potential sellers. To demonstrate your success and credibility, you can also offer case studies, reviews, and testimonials.

8. Evaluate and analyze deals. Once you find potential deals, you need to evaluate and analyze them to determine if they are worth pursuing. You need to do your due diligence and verify the information and data you have, such as property condition, features, location, market value, rental income, expenses, etc. You also need to perform a financial analysis and calculate the key metrics and indicators that measure the profitability and performance of your investments, such as cash flow, cash-on-cash return, cap rate, internal rate of return, etc. You should use tools such as calculators, spreadsheets, and apps to help you with your analysis and comparison. You should also have a set of criteria and standards that you use to filter and rank your deals, and to decide which ones to pursue or pass on.

9. Make and negotiate offers. After you evaluate and analyze your deals, you need to make and negotiate offers to buy the properties. You need to determine how much to offer, based on your analysis, budget, and goals. You also need to decide what terms and conditions to include, such as contingencies, inspections, appraisals, financing, closing date, etc. You should use a standard purchase agreement or contract, and have it reviewed by your real estate agent and attorney. You should also have a proof of funds or earnest money deposit to show your seriousness and commitment.

You should be prepared to negotiate with the seller or their agent, and to make counteroffers or concessions, until you reach a mutually agreeable price and terms. You should also be ready to walk away from a deal if it does not meet your criteria or expectations.

10. Close the deal and manage the property. After you make and negotiate your offer, you need to close the deal and manage the property. You need to complete the necessary steps and paperwork to finalize the transaction, such as title search, title insurance, escrow, closing costs, etc. You also need to secure your financing and pay your lender, seller, and other parties involved. You should have a final walkthrough and inspection of the property, and make sure everything is in order and as agreed. You should also transfer the utilities, keys, and documents to your name. After you close the deal, you need to manage the property, either by yourself or by hiring a property manager. You need to implement your strategy, such as renting, flipping, or holding the property, and execute your plan, such as marketing, leasing marketing, leasing, screening, maintaining, repairing, etc. You need to monitor and optimize your performance and returns, such as collecting rent, paying expenses, tracking income, reporting taxes, etc. You should also have a plan to exit or sell your property, if and when you decide to do so.

These are some of the basic steps to help you get started with real estate investing. However, keep in mind that real estate investing is a complex and dynamic field, and there is no one-size-fits-all approach. You should always do your own research, education, and due diligence before making any investment decisions. You should also consult with qualified professionals, such as your real estate agent, lender, contractor, property manager, accountant, attorney, mentor, or partner, for guidance and advice. Real estate investing can be rewarding, but it also involves risks, challenges, and responsibilities. You should be prepared to face and overcome them, and to learn and grow from your experiences. Happy investing!

# Chapter 3: Financing Your Real Estate Investments

Financing your real estate investments is a crucial step to achieving your goals as an investor. There are many options and strategies to finance your properties, depending on your situation, objectives, and preferences. Here are some of the most common and effective ways to finance your real estate investments:

Cash: Cash is the simplest and most straightforward way to finance your real estate investments. You can use your own savings, sell some of your assets, or partner with someone who has cash to buy properties outright. The advantages of using cash are that you can avoid paying interest, fees, and closing costs, and you can negotiate better deals and discounts with sellers. The disadvantages are that you need to have a lot of cash available, and you limit your leverage and potential returns.

Conventional loans: Conventional loans are mortgages that conform to the standards set by Fannie Mae or Freddie Mac, and are not backed by the government. You can get conventional loans from banks, credit unions, or other lenders, and use them to finance your investment properties. The advantages of conventional loans are that they have lower interest rates, longer terms, and more flexibility than other types of loans.

The disadvantages are that they have stricter qualification criteria, such as credit score, income, debt-to-income ratio, and reserves, and they require higher down payments, usually 20% to 30% of the property value.

Hard money loans: Hard money loans are short-term loans that are secured by the value of the property, and are usually provided by private investors or companies. You can use hard money loans to finance your fix-and-flip projects, or to bridge the gap between buying and selling a property. The advantages of hard money loans are that they are easier to qualify for, faster to obtain, and more flexible than conventional loans. The disadvantages are that they have higher interest rates, fees, and points, and shorter terms, usually 6 to 12 months.

Private money loans: Private money loans are similar to hard money loans, except that they are provided by individuals, such as friends, family, or acquaintances, rather than professional lenders. You can use private money loans to finance any type of real estate investment, as long as you have a good relationship and trust with the lender. The advantages of private money loans are that they have lower interest rates, fees, and points, and more favorable terms and conditions than hard money loans. The disadvantages are that they may involve more emotional and personal risks, and they may not be as reliable or consistent as hard money loans.

Home equity loans: Home equity loans are loans that are based on the difference between the value of your primary residence and the amount you owe on it. You can use home equity loans to finance your investment properties, by borrowing against the equity you have built up in your home. The advantages of home equity loans are that they have lower interest rates and tax benefits than other types of loans, and they allow you to leverage your existing asset. The disadvantages are that you put your primary residence at risk, and you reduce your equity and cash flow.

Online real estate platforms: Online real estate platforms are websites or apps that connect investors to real estate projects, such as crowdfunding, peer-to-peer lending, or syndication. You can use online real estate platforms to finance your real estate investments, by investing in various types of properties and deals, often with lower minimums and fees than traditional methods. The advantages of online real estate platforms are that they offer more access, information, and diversification than other types of financing, and they allow you to invest passively and remotely. The disadvantages are that they involve more platform risks, regulations, and due diligence than other types of financing, and they may have lower control and potential conflicts of interest.

These are some of the most common and effective ways to finance your real estate investments. However, you should always do your own research, education, and due diligence before making any investment decisions. You should also consult with qualified professionals, such as your real estate agent, lender, contractor, property manager, accountant, attorney, mentor, or partner, for guidance and advice. Financing your real estate investments can be challenging, but it can also be rewarding, if you choose the right option and strategy for your situation. Happy investing!

# Chapter 4: Building Your Real Estate Portfolio

1. Determine your investing objectives: Establish your investment objectives and the time range you plan to use to reach them. This will assist you in choosing the risk vs reward strategy you should employ to achieve it. Since real estate investing involves both risk and reward, your willingness to lose some or all of your initial investment in order to achieve your financial objectives will ultimately determine how risk tolerant you are.

2. Start small: It's advisable to begin modestly while constructing your real estate portfolio. You still have a lot to learn about the real estate market, tenant management, and how to raise a property's worth. You can learn from your mistakes and make mistakes without having to risk too much money if you start small.

3. Create the correct relationships: When developing a real estate portfolio, creating the right connections is essential. Developing connections with contractors, real estate brokers, and other investors is part of this. These connections can assist you in locating offers, obtaining funding, and receiving guidance from knowledgeable specialists.

4. Diversify your portfolio: The secret to creating a profitable real estate portfolio is diversification. This entails making investments in several real estate categories, including residential, commercial, and industrial assets, as well as various geographic areas. Diversification aids in distributing risk and optimizing rewards.

5. Remain organized: It's critical to maintain an accurate record of your real estate holdings. This entails tracking your earnings and outlays, maintaining an eye on your financial flow, and maintaining records of your investments. Maintaining organization will assist you in making wise choices and monitoring your money.

# Chapter 5: Managing Your Real Estate Investments

Although it holds great potential, real estate investing requires skillful management to prosper in a changing marketplace. From strategic planning to daily operations, there are many facets of successful management. We'll go over important ideas in this in-depth tutorial to help you make sense of the complex world of real estate investment management.

1. Establishing Unambiguous Goals:

Establish clear objectives for your investments before tackling the complexity of real estate management. Think about things like the length of your investing horizon, your risk tolerance, and the expected returns. As you make decisions throughout the investing lifecycle, these goals will serve as your compass.

2. Due Diligence and Property Selection: A wise choice of properties is the foundation of good management. Assess the property's condition, market trends, and location as part of your comprehensive due diligence. Take into account the neighborhood's infrastructure, future growth possibilities, and potential for appreciation. Some risk mitigation can be achieved later on by taking a careful approach up front.

3. funding Strategies: In order to maximize your capital structure, investigate a variety of funding solutions. Consider possible collaborations, loans, and mortgages. Recognize how interest rates, terms of the loan, and leverage affect your total profits. Real estate investors who want to succeed financially must strike the correct mix between debt and equity.

4. Control of Cash Flow: Real estate investments depend on consistent cash flow. Create a solid plan to pay for utilities, your mortgage, and unforeseen bills. A contingency fund should be established, along with reasonable rental rates and a budget for upkeep of the property. For profitability to continue, there must be a steady positive cash flow.

5. The reduction of vacancies is greatly aided by having good tenant relations and property maintenance. Make sure that tenants are well screened, that maintenance requests are addressed quickly, and that property maintenance is given top priority. As a result of increased lease renewal rates and lower turnover costs, happy renters help to maintain a steady flow of revenue.

6. Insurance and Risk Management: Determine possible hazards related to property ownership and put into practice practical risk-reduction techniques. To guard against unanticipated catastrophes, liability claims, and natural disasters, get comprehensive insurance

coverage. Analyze and revise your risk management strategy on a regular basis to accommodate changing market circumstances.

7. Compliance with Law and Regulation: Keep up with all local, state, and federal laws pertaining to real estate investments. Observe tenant rights, fair housing legislation, and zoning ordinances. Legal experts can help you make sure your property management procedures comply with the law and avoid future legal issues.

8. departure Strategies: Create well-considered departure strategies as part of your long-term planning. In determining whether to sell, refinance, or hang onto the property, take into account the state of the market, possible appreciation, and your financial objectives. To optimize profits and adjust to shifting market conditions, it is imperative to have a well-defined exit strategy.

9. Diversifying Your Portfolio: To reduce risk and increase overall stability, diversify your real estate holdings. Investigate various real estate kinds, regions, and financial approaches. In addition to offering protection from regional market downturns, a diversified portfolio offers a more resilient and balanced investing strategy.

10. Never-ending Education and Adjustment: Since real estate markets change all the time, investors have to be educated and flexible. Participate in ongoing learning about new technologies, investing approaches, and market trends.

For long-term success in the fast-paced real estate market, the ability to adjust and adjust to shifting market conditions and industry advancements is critical.

# Chapter 6: Maximizing Your Real Estate Returns

1. Recognize your ROI (return on investment): Return on investment (ROI) is a metric that is computed as a percentage of the initial investment. It is crucial to real estate investing since it makes it easier for buyers to evaluate potential investments and select the most lucrative one. Real estate investment trusts (REITs), commercial real estate, rental properties, and fix-and-flip properties are among the several kinds of real estate investments that yield a return on investment. Every investment kind has pros and cons of its own, and the return on investment might change based on the kind of investment. The location, state of the property, rental revenue and costs, leverage and financing, taxes, and depreciation are some of the variables that affect return on investment (ROI) in real estate. You may make more informed judgments about when to buy, sell, or retain your investments if you are aware of your return on investment.

2. Purchase properties with added value: Properties with potential for improvement to raise their value are known as value-add properties. This may entail making improvements to the landscaping, adding amenities, or remodeling the property.

Investing in properties with added value can raise the value of your home and your rental income, which can result in larger profits.

3. Think about investing in real estate crowdfunding: You can invest in real estate projects with less money by using real estate crowdfunding. It enables investors to combine their funds in order to participate in bigger real estate ventures. This can provide investors access to larger real estate transactions that they might not otherwise be able to finance. Platforms for real estate crowdfunding often include a range of investment options, such as debt, hybrid, and equity investments.

4. Maximize your rental revenue: The secret to optimizing your returns as a property owner is to maximize your rental income. This may entail bringing down your costs, locating excellent renters, and raising your rental rates. You may reduce costs and boost rental income with the aid of competent tenant management.

5. Remain current with market trends: To maximize your earnings, you must remain current with market trends. This entails remaining abreast of market developments, evaluating market data, and tracking market trends. This will assist you in determining the best time to buy, sell, or keep onto your investments.

# Chapter 7: Retiring Early with Real Estate

1. Get started early: It's best to begin investing in real estate as soon as possible. Investing in real estate is a long-term strategy that calls for effort and patience. Starting early allows you to capitalize on compound interest and gradually accumulate a sizeable real estate portfolio

2. Purchase rental properties: Purchasing rental homes is an excellent method of obtaining passive income. If you own rental properties, you can utilize the money you get from renters to cover other costs, such as your mortgage. You can benefit from a consistent passive income source that can enable you to retire early once your mortgage is paid off.

3. Diversify your portfolio: A successful real estate portfolio requires diversification. This entails making investments in many property kinds, including commercial, industrial, and residential buildings, as well as various geographic regions. To disperse risk and optimize returns, use diversification.

4. Maximize your rental income: If you are a property owner, the secret to increasing your profits is to make the most of your rentals.

Finding suitable renters, cutting costs, and raising rental rates are some ways to achieve this. You can save costs and increase rental income with the aid of effective tenant management.

5. Consider crowdfunding for real estate: Investing in real estate projects with a limited budget is possible through crowdfunding. It enables investors to combine their funds to make larger investments in real estate projects. Through this, investors may be able to participate in larger real estate transactions that they otherwise might not have access to. Crowdfunding platforms for real estate usually include a range of investment options, such as debt, hybrid, and equity investments.

6. Know how to calculate your return on investment (ROI) ROI stands for return on investment, and it is expressed as a percentage of the initial investment. It is crucial to real estate investing because it facilitates the comparison of various ventures and the selection of the most lucrative one. A variety of real estate investment strategies can yield a return on investment, such as commercial real estate, rental properties, fix-and-flip buildings, and real estate investment trusts (REITs). There are benefits and drawbacks to any kind of investment, and the return on investment might change based on the kind of investment. A number of variables, including location, property condition, rental revenue and expenses, leverage and financing, taxes, and depreciation, affect return on investment (ROI)

in real estate. Making wise decisions on when to buy, sell, or hold your investments will be made easier if you are aware of your return on investment.

7. Remain current with market trends: Optimizing your returns requires keeping up of market developments. This entails monitoring market developments, assessing market data, and remaining current with trends in the industry. This will enable you to choose wisely when to sell, buy, or hold onto your money.

# Conclusion

In "Retire Early with Real Estate," it is made clear that wise real estate investing is a means of achieving financial freedom as well as a tool for increasing wealth. The delicate guidelines of property selection, careful management, and flexibility in response to market conditions pave the way for an early retirement.

It's evident from our exploration of the nuances of real estate that making wise decisions along with continuing knowledge is the key to achieving an early retirement. Investors are able to establish a strong basis for financial independence through defining clear goals, carefully choosing properties, and negotiating the challenges of financing.

One cannot stress the importance of tenant relations and efficient cash flow management enough. Building strong tenant connections guarantees property stability and long-term revenue streams, while positive cash flow supports the retiree's lifestyle. The foundation of a safe and robust real estate portfolio is made up of these pillars, risk management procedures, and adherence to regulatory requirements.

Not to mention, it is imperative to keep a diverse portfolio and have clear exit options. Investors can profit from market conditions when they exit their investments with consideration, whether they choose to sell, refinance, or hold.

Increased overall portfolio stability and protection against economic swings are two benefits of diversification in property kinds and geographic areas.

The real estate market is dynamic, requiring constant learning and adaptability. To ensure long-term success, it is essential to keep up with market trends, embrace technical innovations, and modify plans in response to changes in the economy. Since the journey of a retiree is dynamic, the capacity for innovation and pivoting assures adaptability to shifts.

Closing "Retire Early with Real Estate," the message is quite clear: real estate can help make early retirement a reality. Combining strategic planning, proactive problem-solving, and a wealth of information is required. By putting the advice in this guide to use, investors can design a future in which early retirement and financial independence coexist, opening up new avenues for opportunity and realizing lifelong goals.

# Gratitude & Acknowledgment:

To All of You Readers:

We are coming to the close of our study of "Retire Early with Real Estate," and I would want to take this opportunity to thank you for selecting this book to help you on your path to retirement. It is a testament to your dedication to a better and more secure future that you have taken the time to carefully read these pages.

I hope the knowledge and viewpoints offered in these chapters have given you useful tools and ideas for using real estate to finance an early retirement. The ideas that have been addressed are in accordance with your goal of financial independence, and I have no doubt that the techniques that have been described can help you achieve your goal of a happy and independent retirement.

Please help me by leaving a review of "Retire Early with Real Estate" on Amazon if you think it was a helpful resource. In addition to attesting to the book's applicability, your positive evaluations help other readers who are interested in learning more about early retirement and real estate investing.

Thank you so much for taking the time to write a review; your input is really helpful.

I hope your real estate ventures succeed and that this book's lessons will help you stay on the right track toward financial independence and early retirement.

I am grateful that you joined me on this adventure.

With best wishes,

[**J.B. BLACKWOOD**]